Richard Mayde

Ancient Egypt

Richard Mayde

Ancient Egypt

ISBN/EAN: 9783337240141

Printed in Europe, USA, Canada, Australia, Japan

Cover: Foto ©ninafisch / pixelio.de

More available books at **www.hansebooks.com**

ANCIENT EGYPT.

ILLUSTRATED.

NEW YORK:
DODD, MEAD, AND COMPANY,

1. The Pyramids......................FRONTISPI
2. Lotus Flower...........................PAGE
3. Making Bricks.............................
4. Making Bricks.............................
5. Ancient Egyptian Boat......................
6. Drawing Water from the Nile................
7. Watering the Fields.........................
8. Modern Nile Boat...........................
9. Ark and Priests of Nilus....................
10. Egyptian Water Wheel.......................
11. Egyptian Locust............................
12. Banners of the Egyptians...................
13. Fishing in a Canal.........................
14. Egyptian Field.............................
15. Fruit Basket...............................

16. Wine Jar ....
17. Egyptian Cup ....
18. Dining Chair......................
19. Chair.............................
20. Mirror............................
21. Carved Box ....
22. Basin and Pitcher.................
23. Stone Polisher....................
24. Toy Crocodile.....................
25. Modern Slave Boat on the Nile ....
26. Egyptian High Priest ....
27. Looking South from Philæ ....
28. Day of Judgment ....
29. Ru'ns at Philæ......................
30. The Sacred Bull... ....
31. Resurrection of the Body..............
32. Priest preparing Mummy for Burial .....
33. Egyptian Jars.................
34. Mummy Case ....
35. Ancient Rock-cut Tomb...............
36. Interior of Rock-cut Tomb............
37. Pyramids of Memphis.................

LIST OF ILLUSTRATIONS. 7

		PAGE
38.	Court of an Egyptian Temple	88
39.	Ruins at Karnak	90
40.	The Sphinx	91
41.	Luxor from the River	95
42.	A Sphinx	100
43.	Ruined Avenue of Sphinxes	101
44.	Ancient Temple	103
45.	Ramessids at Luxor	105
46.	The Colossi	109
47.	Ruins of Temple of Rameses	113
48.	Statue of Osymandyas	117

CHAPTER I.

Lotus flower.

IF we look on the map of Africa we shall find in the very northeastern part, a country that is set down as Egypt. A long and narrow country it is, and throughout its whole length flows a great river, while the fertile fields on its banks lie like a long and narrow green ribbon, through the vast deserts that surround it on every side. Such in reality is the habitable country of Egypt:—a belt of fertile land lying on the banks of the river, and made fertile by the overflow of its waters.

And yet this country so apparently insignificant in size was the home of a great and mighty nation far back in the very beginning of history. When we read in the book of Genesis of the times of Abraham, that great shepherd, and of his vast flocks and herds, and how the angel of the Lord came to his tent to bring to him the promise that he should be the father of a great nation, we seem to be reading of the very earliest days of the world. And yet when Abraham went down to Egypt to find pasturage for his cattle, he found a people who had lived there for centuries, ruled over by kings, the builders of great palaces and massive temples to the strange gods whom they worshipped.

Fortunately we have preserved to us many of the records of these early ages.

Making Bricks.

How, you ask, can that be? How could these records have been preserved for four thousand years, and on what could they have been written before the invention of parchment and pen. The parchment was the hard granite rock, and the pen the workman's chisel, and from this it has happened that these records have been preserved, while those of nations centuries] have utterly disappeared.

Of course they were not in writing, for it was many hundreds of years after this

Making Bricks; from Ancient Egyptian Monument.

that the alphabet was discovered. They are written in a language that all can read—in pictures, such as the two, representing brickmaking, here given.

How was it that Egypt came thus early

to be so mighty an empire? It was largely owing to the position of the country. In the early days, the art of navigation was almost unknown. Ships were of the frailest character, and in them the timid sailor dared not venture out of sight of land. But the whole country of Egypt was traversed by a mighty river, down whose broad and placid current could float in safety the rudest vessels, bearing the grain and fruits of one section to another—bringing down the huge building stones for the temples and pyramids, or carrying the gold from far Ethiopia to Thebes, the great and mighty capital.

For nine months out of the twelve a strong wind blows southward through the Nile valley, from sunrise to sunset, and so the early navigators returning up the stream, down which they had floated, could hoist the sails, and make good progress during the day, anchoring at night, when the wind died

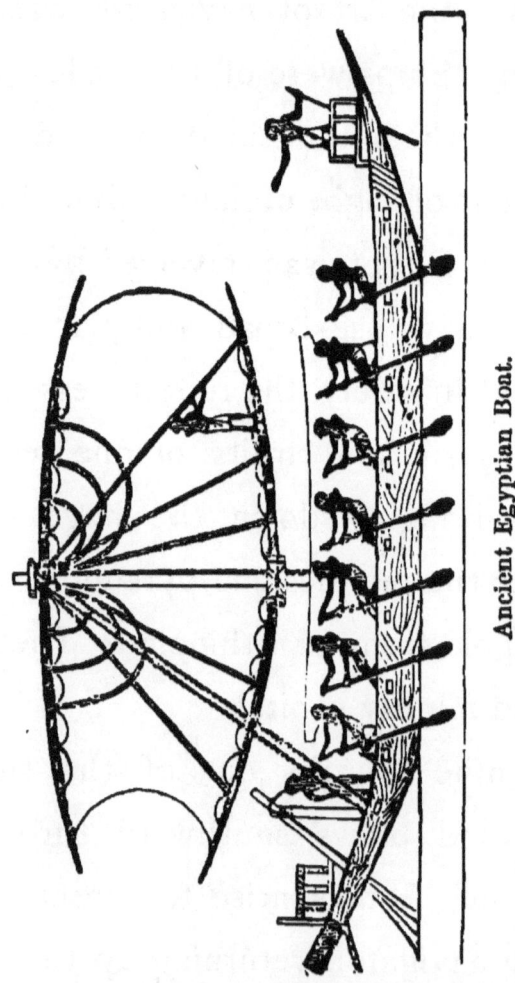

Ancient Egyptian Boat.

away. In this way, intercourse was held

between all parts of the country, and as a natural result, the arts of peace flourished. The husbandman was far more intent in gathering a rich and certain harvest from the fertile soil, than in going abroad to seek the uncertain booty of war; and laws and government speedily followed.

The valley of the Nile is, as we have said, the only habitable part of Egypt, for this is the only part that is ever watered. In this country rain never falls;—the river only is the source of all life, and where its waters cannot reach, are only desert sands. About the middle of June, the waters of the Nile begin to rise, and continue rising till they reach the height of about twenty feet. The whole valley during the months of August, September, and October, is under water, while the villages, built on raised mounds, rise above the flood, like islands in a vast lake. The people watch with eagerness for the coming of the waters, and its first appearance is

Drawing water from the Nile.

hailed with the firing of guns, and the shouts of the crowd who line the river banks.

The thrifty husbandman has dug canals, in order that the life-giving water may reach and moisten the dry sands, that would otherwise go untilled, and, with the help of rude

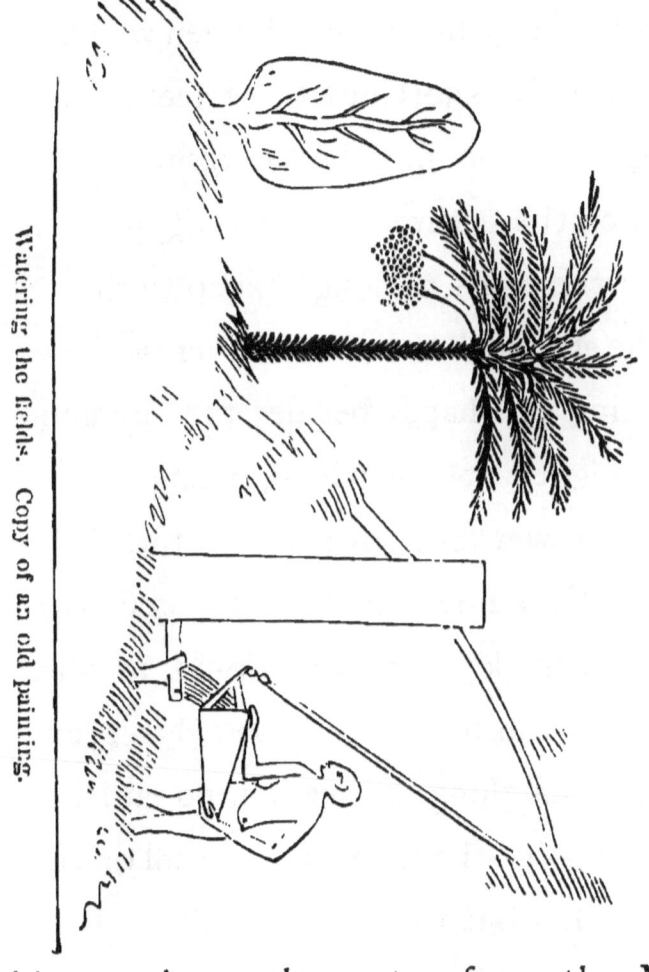

Watering the fields. Copy of an old painting.

machinery, draws the water from the Nile and pours it on the thirsty soil.

The rise of the river each year varies but a few inches, and the eagerness with which it is watched may be imagined when we know that should it fall short but a few feet of its usual height, famine must be the result.

For these three months Egypt is a vast lake; the boats no longer keep to the channel of the stream, but sail boldly across the waters, coasting perhaps beside the pyramids, or the mighty colossi which, rising out of the waves, tower far above the boatmen's heads.

In November the fields are again bare, but covered thickly with a rich mud, in which the husbandman has but to sow his seed. No weary ploughing is needed, no enriching the wasted soil—the river has done all this for him, and he has but to reap the fruit of its labor. Two crops are sown and gathered before the sun has parched the ground so thoroughly

Nile Boats.

moistened by the overflow. All through our winter, the fields of Egypt are green with the growing crops, or golden with the harvest; but when with us the spring has come and our fields grow green, those of Egypt are parched and waste, till again the rushing waters shall fertilize them anew. The old Greek historian Herodotus tells of the amazement of the Egyptian priests, when they learned that all Greece was watered by rain from heaven, and not, as their own country, inundated by rivers. "Some day," they said, "the Greeks will be disappointed of their grand hope, and then they will be wretchedly hungry," evidently thinking that any people that depended on rain alone to moisten the soil, depended on a very frail hope indeed.

We now know that the yearly rise of the river is caused by the rains in Abyssinia, which, pouring down the mountain sides, swell the mighty flood that rushes onward till it reaches the Mediterranean; but to the ancient Egyptians, who did not know this, the yearly coming of the flood was miraculous indeed.

Ark and Priests of Nilus.

Should it fail for a single year, the green fields would become deserts, and the nation must perish with famine. It was the source of food—of life, and the mystery which shrouded its coming only increased their wonder and awe. To them it appeared a god, and they worshipped it as such. Priests were appointed, who presided over the sacrifices offered it, and in every way it was treated with the utmost reverence.

The Nile Valley, which was thus made fertile by the overflow of the river, is indeed a narrow strip of land. In its widest part, except at the delta where it discharges into the Mediterranean, it is only ten and three-quarter miles in width, while the average breadth of the cultivated land is only a little over four miles.

Yet this narrow belt supported a vast population. Herodotus declares that, in his day, there were twenty thousand cities, while the total number of inhabitants was seven millions. How all these people lived we shall see as we go on.

HOME LIFE OF THE EGYPTIANS.

Egyptian Water Wheel

CHAPTER II.

Egyptian Locust.

THE Egyptian house was thoroughly adapted to the climate. In a country wherein rain never falls, and where dampness is unknown, we can easily imagine that the lower classes would live almost entirely out of doors. And so we find that their houses were simply enclosures, of which only a part was covered over, while the space thus enclosed was used almost entirely for a granary or store-room. The roof was finished off flat, and on it the family always slept at night.

Of course such simple houses as these could only be occupied by the very poor. In the towns they were built of rough brick, were several stories in height, and joined together as in cities in our own day. Over the doorway was generally some inscription, such as "The Good House," or some symbol of good omen. The door was often of rare wood, or stained to imitate rare wood, while the exterior was stuccoed, and painted in the many bright colors in which the Egyptian delighted.

The house-top, as in all Eastern countries, was a favorite place of resort, and here the women doubtless held long gossips with one another. At least this was the case, if we may believe a story which the modern Egyptian tells, and which he claims has come down from the time of the Pharaohs. It is as follows:

"A man digging in his vineyard, having

found a jar full of gold, ran home with joy to announce his good fortune to his wife; but, as he reflected on the way that women could not be always trusted with secrets, and that he might lose a treasure which of right belonged to the king, he thought it better to test her discretion. As soon, therefore, as he had entered the house, he called her to him, and saying that he had something of great importance to tell her, asked if she was sure she could keep a secret. 'Oh yes,' was the ready answer, 'when did you ever know me betray one? What is it?' 'Well then— but you are sure you won't mention it?' 'Have I not told you so--why be so tiresome —what is it?' 'Now, as you promise me, I will tell you. A most singular thing happens to me. Every morning I lay an egg,' at the same time producing one from beneath his cloak 'What! an egg! Extraordinary.' 'Yes, it is indeed, but mind you don't mention it.' 'Oh! no; I shall say nothing about it, I promise you.' 'No! I feel sure you won't;' and so saying he left the house. No sooner gone, than his wife ran up to the terrace, and finding a neighbor on the adjoining roof, she beckoned to her, and with great caution said, 'Oh! my sister, such a curious thing happens to my husband, but you are sure you won't tell anybody.' 'No! no! what is it? do tell me.' 'Every morning he lays ten eggs.' 'What! ten eggs!' 'Yes, and he has shown them to me, is it not strange? but mind you say nothing about it;' and away she went down stairs. It was not long before another woman came up on the next terrace, and the story was told in the same way, by the wife's friend, with a similar promise of secrecy, only with the variation of twenty instead of ten eggs, till one neighbor after another to whom the the story was intrusted, had increased them to a hundred. It was not long before the husband heard it also, and the supposed egg-layer, learning how his story

Banners of the Egyptians.

had spread, was persuaded not to risk his treasure, by trusting his wife with the real secret."

The homes of the rich were very varied in shape, but were in almost every case built around a central and open court, and upheld by columns, through which the breezes found free passage. In the court were often fountains, while the pavement was kept from being overheated, by being continually sprinkled with water. The chief entrance, or hallway, through which the visitor entered, was frequently hung with gayly colored banners.

In the country, where the villas could spread over more space, the grounds were often of great size, including orchards and vineyards, large canals and ponds, which were supplied with water from the river, and stocked with fish, offering not only a place for boating, but a fine fishing ground whenever the master felt inclined for sport.

Granaries, too, were enclosed, and the yards in which were kept the cattle, while beyond all, lay the fields with the toiling laborers.

Flowers were everywhere raised in the greatest quantities, the Egyptians even going so far as to exact them in tribute from conquered nations. Vast beds were spread out

Fishing in one of the Canals. Old Painting.

in every direction, and the servants continually replaced within doors those that were withered, with fresh ones from the garden. The lotus was especially a favorite, and appears in thousands of sculptures on the sacred buildings and tombs.

Egyptian field. Copy of an old painting.

We can easily see that a people who had become so passionately fond of flowers, could not have been a warlike and barbarous race, the first conquerors of the soil, but must have passed through years of civilization. Consequently we expect to find in their houses many indications of refinement. Nor are we disappointed.

Both the sculptures and the accounts of the earliest travellers assure us that the rich lived in a condition of luxury unknown at the present day. The newly arrived guest was met by slaves, who, removing his dusty sandals, presented him water in golden

Fruit Basket of Egypt.

Wine Jar.

bowls, to bathe his feet. When ushered into the apartment to which he had per-

Egyptian Cup.

haps been invited to dine, a bouquet of flowers was given him, while a necklace of flowers was hung about his neck. Wine was handed him in golden cups, and while the guests waited for dinner, they were entertained with music performed by hired musicians.

The room was furnished with carpets, and

A dining chair of Egypt.

some of the chairs and other articles of furniture were made in the richest way, while others, of course, such as here illustrated, were of the simplest form. One of our illustrations, as will be seen, shows a chair that is very similar to the camp chair of daily use to-day. Vases stood about, filled with flowers;—on all sides were flowers; while their pleasant perfumes filled the air.

At the close of the meal, a singular custom was observed. A figure of the god Osiris, carved in the shape of a mummy, some twelve inches in height, was passed from guest to guest, to remind them that however proper it might be to enjoy the good things of this world, there was yet a hereafter, for which each must be prepared. The thought of death was not an unpleasant one to them,

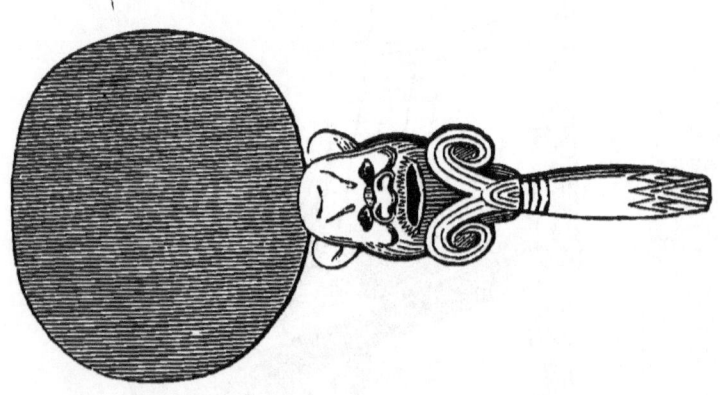

and they were so little moved by it, as to frequently place the mummy of a departed relative at the table among the guests.

If we were familiar enough with the family to pass into the inner rooms, we should see many indications of taste. Here, lying upon the lady's dressing table, is a mirror whose handle is carved into the image of some god; lying next it we find an inlaid box, perhaps used for holding her jewelry or other article of the toilet, while the golden bowl and pitcher seem to vary but little in shape from those made of more common material which are in use at the present day.

In all the pictures we have of family life among the ancient Egyptians, the women are always present, and always on perfect equality with the men. How sure a proof this of civilization, only one who has travelled in Eastern lands, and has seen the low estimation in which 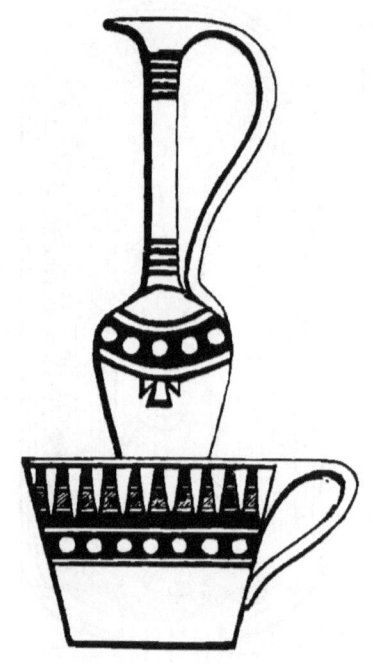 women are held, can really feel. The Arab of to-day, when by chance he mentions the name of his wife, follows it with the expression, "ajellak Allah," "may God elevate you" above the contamination of such a subject; precisely the words he would say, if by chance he should speak the name of a dog or any unclean thing.

The Egyptians had many games which have descended to us:—for instance one now very common in Italy, called moira, was well known to them. In this one person suddenly throws forward several fingers of each hand, while his opponent is obliged to guess instantly the number which they together make. Chess, too, seems to have been a very common amusement, while they had also a game in

Stone Polisher; an Egyptian Toy.

which two persons, each equipped with a stick terminating in a hook, tried by skilful movements to catch away from the other a small hoop. The game of ball was also a favorite, and seems to have been often played by ladies, while they were accomplished in the art of keeping in the air at the same time three, four, or even more balls. Nor were the children forgotten. Here are representations of two mechanical toys which, doubtless, amused the little ones of long ago, as much as the more elaborate ones their successors enjoy. The mouth of the crocodile works

with a string, and shuts with a snap when this is pulled.

When more active amusement was needed, the Egyptian found it in hunting and fishing. The edges of the desert bordering on the fertile valley of the Nile, abounded in game. Gazelles and the wild ox were sometimes hunted down with dogs, or barbacans were formed, into which bodies of men drove the game for miles around. Lions, too, were fierce and numerous, if we may believe a statement of Amunoph III., in which he boasts that in a single day he killed one hundred and two. The Egyptian not only hunted the lion, but he tamed the young cubs and taught them to hunt for him, just as now in India the cubs of the leopard are trained to a similar service. The hyena, the pest of the shepherd, was also hunted, and traps were set for it, in which it had often the misfortune to fall, when it was brought muzzled into the village, amid the rejoicings of the farmers. Probably, however, the sport that afforded the most satisfaction, as well for the difficulty of its pursuit as the value of its prize, was the chase of the ostrich. Its feathers were emblematic of truth, and the highest officials, on occasions of state, were accustomed to adorn themselves with them; and so highly were they valued, that they were exacted as tribute from conquered nations. In addition to all this, the Nile banks were the homes of thousands of birds, whose pursuit afforded many hours of sport to the enthusiastic hunter.

The food of the richer classes was beef, game, and fish from the river, but a country so small as Egypt, and so densely populated, could of course afford animal food for the rich only. The lower classes lived almost entirely on vegetables, which the Nile Valley produced in the greatest abundance. The Israelites, when they had made their escape from bondage, and were marching through the desert, looked back longingly to the onions, the leeks, and the garlic they had left behind them.

The occupations of the Egyptians were many. The nobility seem to have chosen either the army or the priesthood; but when we come to the common people, there were many pursuits followed. A curious law, it is said, compelled every one to follow the occupation of his father; but though this was not perhaps strictly true, it was true that after a man had chosen his trade, he was not allowed to change it.

As might be expected in a country so situated as Egypt, the occupation of husbandman was one of no mean character. We have already shown how the Nile fertilized the land, and how he had but to sow the seed in the waiting soil. Wheat and barley were largely grown, and the grain was threshed by oxen trampling on it, or dragging over it a rude instrument. On one of the sculptures we have such a scene represented, while over it is written the song of the men to the laboring animals :

> "Thresh for yourselves, O oxen!
> Thresh for yourselves ;
> Thresh for yourselves, O oxen !
> Thresh for yourselves.
> Measures for yourselves,
> Measures for your masters ;
> Measures for yourselves,
> Measures for your masters."

Shepherds, however, were looked upon by the Egyptians as following the most degraded occupation of all. Joseph tells his brethren, when they are about to appear before Pharaoh, to, by no means, state plainly their calling, " for every shepherd is an abomination to the Egyptians."

We are surprised to find that many things which we have been accustomed to think modern inventions were well known to the Egyptians. Thus glass-making was known to them four thousand years ago, and they reached a skill in its manufacture that is totally unknown at the present day. Wilkinson speaks of a mosaic of glass, in which the fineness of the design was such, that some parts, such as the feathers of birds, could only be satisfactorily studied under a magnifying glass. They succeeded, too, in imitating precious stones, and though we can hardly think this a very noble use of their skill, it yet shows to what extent civilization had gone in those early days, since it is not till the arts of peace are well-established, that the desire for articles of personal adornment comes. The looms of Egypt were widely known, and their linen was largely exported. At home, too, large quantities must have been used, for linen formed the dress of the Egyptian living, and in it his body was wrapped for burial. Workers in leather are shown on the sculptures, fullers too, and potters, while the luxurious furniture of the houses of the rich, of which we have spoken, gave occupation to the carpenter and upholsterer. The Egyptians were skilled workers in the precious metals. The mines of Nubia afforded gold, and were carried on by the government; and the laborers were either convicts or prisoners taken in war. Their fate was indeed a hard one. Bound in fetters, men and women alike, they were driven on by taskmasters speaking a foreign tongue, without regard to their sufferings, till death brought a merciful relief.

RELIGION OF THE EGYPTIANS.

Modern Slave-boat on the Nile.

CHAPTER III.

ORIGINALLY the Egyptian reverenced one God only whose likeness was never represented, "he being worshipped in silence." His characteristics, however, were represented by visible shapes.

Egyptian High Priest offering flowers.

To make this plainer,—when they thought of God as exercising his power in different ways, they represented him by figures, to each of which they gave a distinguishing name.

Thus if they thought of him as a creator, he was called Pthah, and his figure was always accompanied by a smaller figure of Truth; as the principle of generation, or the life-giver, he was called Khem, and so on; in short; they expressed in pictures each of the various attributes of the Deity which we distinguish by such words as The Almighty, The Everlasting. Now while the educated could understand this, and regard these as emblems of the one All-father, the lower classes soon came to regard them as separate gods, and to pay divine honors to a host of deities, whose origin was lost in a mass of tradition and fable. Not only this, but if they perceived in any animal qualities which were associated with any of these deities, they considered the animal sacred, and so we have the curious spectacle of a nation paying reverence to the bull, and holding in sacred estimation cats and beetles. To such an extent was this the case, that the Greeks declared that it was easier, on the banks of the Nile, to find a god than a man.

These many gods were not held in equal estimation; a deity who was the chief object of worship in one part of the country, was totally ignored in another. Thus Pthah was reverenced in Memphis, Amun Ra, the sun-god, in Heliopolis, Pasht, the goddess of chastity, at Bubastis. This was true, too, of animals, those held sacred in one section being considered worthy of no regard, or even as symbols of evil, in another.

There were, however, two exceptions to what we have just said. Osiris and Isis were worshipped in every part of Egypt alike, and everywhere honored as the greatest of the gods. The island of Philæ, in the Nile, was especially consecrated to them, and in the eyes of the people, was the most sacred spot in the world. They looked upon it as the Mohammedan looks upon Mecca, or as the Christian upon the scenes amid which our Lord lived and moved; and the Egyptian could give no more solemn oath than "by him—unnamed and unnameable—who sleeps in Philæ." They believed that no bird dared fly over so holy a spot, and here they erected a most magnificent temple to their god. The destroying fury of the Persian conqueror has left but a portion standing of this beautiful shrine. Here we have traced upon the walls in the many chapels—for the building was of immense size—the mythological history of Osiris. He was believed to be the son of Nu and Seb, the brother and husband

Looking South from Temple roof at Philæ.

of Isis, his queen, and was put to death by Typhon, but in the spirit world he was restored to life, and made the judge of the dead. This, however, was but the myth of a later day; in the earlier and purer worship of the Egyptians, he personified the divine goodness. It was believed that he came on earth to bless mankind, but that he was vanquished and put to death by the power of evil. He rose from the dead to become the judge of all mankind. On the next page is a picture showing how the Egyptians kept before the people the idea of the world to come and the day of judgment.

Osiris sits upon his throne, with a flail to punish or staff to guide, as the soul before him is accepted or found wanting. The sacred lotus flower is on the altar. The terrible dog —the Cerberus of the Greeks—the guardian of the gates, waits his decision. Thoth, god of letters, stands with ready pen to record the decision. The dog-headed Anubis places a vase representing good actions, or the heart of the deceased, in one scale, and the figure of truth in the other. Horus assists in the weighing. The spirit holds up praying hands, waiting between two figures of truth, the sentence that shall assign to it endless happiness, or consign it to endless woe.

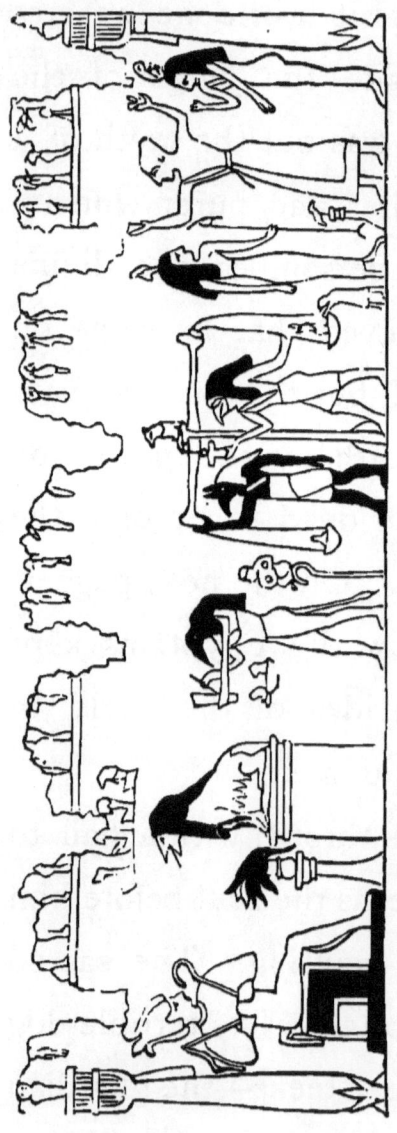

Remains of Small Temple at Philæ.

Close by this temple of Osiris at Philæ was a small one, dedicated to his queen and sister, Isis.

If we may believe the accounts of modern travellers, the Egyptians, in selecting the island of Philæ as the home for their gods, chose a spot of wonderful beauty. A late writer speaks of it as "the most strangely wild and beautiful spot he ever beheld. For all around the traveller tower up vast masses of gloomy rocks, piled one upon the other in wildest confusion;—some of them as it were skeletons of pyramids; others requiring only a few strokes of giant labor to form colossal statues that might have startled the Anakim. Here spreads a deep drift of silvery sand, fringed by rich verdure and purple blossoms; there, a grove of palms, intermingled with the flowering acacia; and there, through vistas of craggy cliffs and gloomy foliage, gleams a calm blue lake, with the sacred island in the midst, green to the water's edge, except where the walls of the old temple city are reflected."

In Memphis, too, the worship of Osiris was carried on with great pomp, but here he was reverenced in the form of a living bull, Apis. It was claimed that this bull was divinely born, its mother being a cow of wonderful beauty, selected by the gods for this high office, and many were the honors bestowed upon it. It was kept in a temple built for it, its food was selected with the greatest care, it was forbidden to drink the water of the Nile, since this was supposed to have a peculiarly fattening quality, and the Egyptians believed that " the body should sit light upon the soul," and in every way its comfort was provided for. The limit of its life was twenty-five years. If it died before this, its body was embalmed and, placed in a huge sarcophagus, was laid away in tombs with those of its predecessors. If the bull lived to be twenty-five, it was then secretly killed.

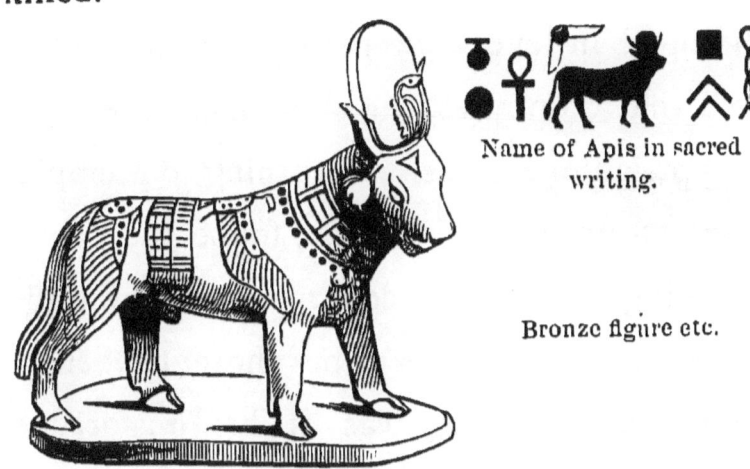

Name of Apis in sacred writing.

Bronze figure etc.

When the Apis was dead, the people gave way to great lamentations. Priests, selected for the purpose, immediately set out to find a new one, which was to be made known by certain distinctive marks on his body. When found he was fed for forty days in a house facing the rising sun, and allowed to be seen only by women. At the expiration of this time he was placed in a golden boat, and carried on the Nile to Memphis. When the report was spread that a new Apis was found, the people ceased their lamentations, and indulged in every expression of joy. It is said that Cambyses, the Persian conqueror of Egypt, on one occasion returning to Memphis after an unsuccessful battle, found the people rejoicing over the discovery of a new Apis. In his anger at defeat, he chose to believe that their rejoicing was at his misfortune, and summoned the priests before him, with the sacred bull. Rushing upon the bull, he wounded him with his sword, exclaiming that he would see if a tame god had come to earth. The superstitious people believed that all the subsequent misfortunes of this prince were in punishment for this sacrilegious act. On festal days the bull was led at the head of processions, surrounded by a band of priests to keep back the people who came forth from their houses to greet it, and strew flowers in its way, while children who breathed its breath were thought to have the power of foretelling the future.

The service of all these many gods, and the care of the temples erected in their honor, required a vast number of priests. To the higher classes in Egypt there seem to have been but two paths open—the army and the priesthood. The king was, at the same time, the head of the civil government and the chief high priest; but the sons of the nobility could choose only one or the other of these two occupations.

The priests enjoyed many privileges.

Their property was not subject to taxes Their expenses were paid by the state. And, though they undoubtedly erred in not directing aright the worship of the people—allowing them to reverence animals rather than the God of whom they were but symbols—they yet showed in their lives decided examples of self-restraint and self-control. In the care of their persons they were most exact. They bathed four times a day, and every second day shaved from head to foot. Their food was of the simplest, and they never allowed themselves indulgence in the pleasures of the table, for they never lost sight of their great principle, that the body should sit light upon the soul. Nor did they believe that any sanctity was connected with celibacy. They married, and had their families about them.

The Egyptian believed implicitly in the resurrection of the body, even going so far as to place with it at burial, seeds of grain and farming tools, in order that the returning spirit might have the necessary aids in again beginning life. Their resurrection was not that of the Christian, who believes that the natural body shall rise a spiritual body. They believed that the spirit must return to the body which it occupied in life, and should that body be destroyed, no future life could be enjoyed. In the next picture the god Anubis is removing the cloths from the man long dead, while the soul, represented as a winged spirit, is about to return, entering through the mouth.

In consequence of this belief, every care was taken so to prepare the body that it might be uninjured through the ages that must elapse before the spirit should return to its former home. The Egyptian hoarded and toiled through life that his final resting-place might be one that should defy decay.

Resurrection of the body.

As soon as a death occurred, the females of the household, their heads and faces covered with mud, rushed wildly, with naked breasts, through the streets, striking themselves and moaning aloud.

Friends and relatives joined them, and if the dead man were a person of position, strangers followed to show their respect. Hired mourners, too, added to the lamentations.

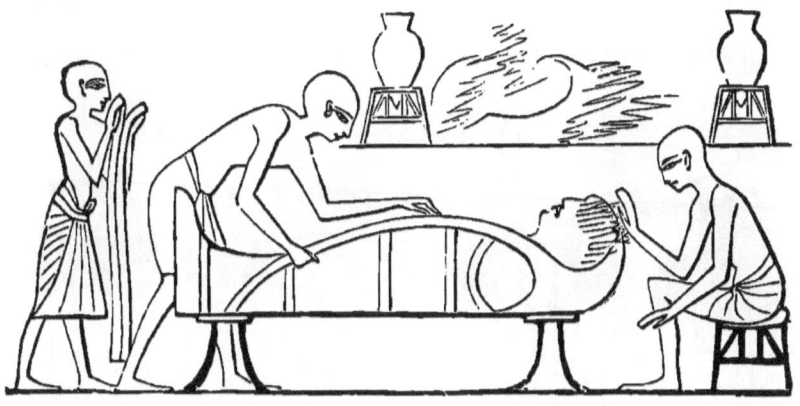

Priests preparing Mummy for Burial.

The body was at once embalmed with the greatest care, this being exclusively the work of the priests; and, wrapped in many folds of linen cloth, was made ready for its long sleep.

The process of embalming took seventy days, and was one on which the greatest care was exercised. Several different methods are known to have been in use, varying in expense according to the means employed. Often the intestines were removed, and the empty space was filled with bitumen or some similar substance, while the intestines themselves were deposited in four vases, which

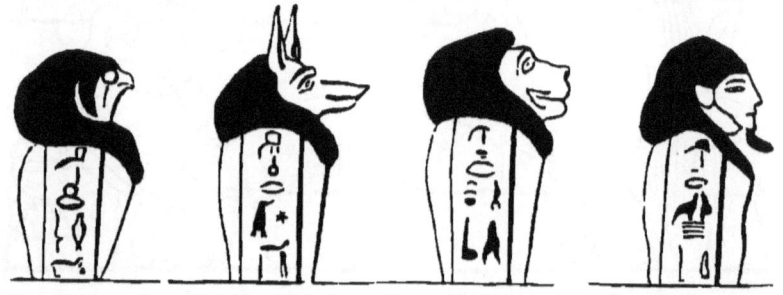

Four Egyptian Jars containing the perishable parts of the Mummy.

were placed in the tomb containing the sarcophagus.

These vases, as here shown, each terminated in a head, and were of a peculiar character, and to each a particular part of the perishable part of the mummy was always assigned. Burial did not always at once follow embalming; for sometimes the mummy, after being delivered to its friends, was kept in the house by them for months, where, placed in a richly painted case, it was set upright against the wall. When the appointed day for the funeral had come, and the procession had reached the place of sepulture, a singular custom was observed. Judges being provided, it was open to any one to bring charges against the dead. Should these charges not be approved, a severe punishment was afflicted on the false accuser, but should it be shown that the dead man had led an evil life, burial was refused, and the mummy was returned to its friends. Great was the grief and shame among the relatives, for this was the greatest dishonor that could befall them.

In such a case as this, the mummy was generally kept in the house, a closet being constructed for this purpose. In such way too, were kept the mummies of those that had died in debt, until their children had released them by the payment of their creditors. "It was indeed," says an old historian, "most solemnly established in Egypt, that parents and ancestors should have a more

marked token of respect paid them by their family after they had been transferred to their everlasting habitations. Hence originated the custom of depositing the bodies of their deceased parents as pledges for the payment of borrowed money: those who failed to redeem these pledges being subject to the

Ancient rock-cut Tomb.

heaviest disgrace, and deprived of burial after their own death."

The various districts of Egypt differed somewhat in their modes of burial. Opposite Thebes, where the line of hills comes down near the river, the limestone rock was carved out into tombs.

Thousands of them cover the hill-sides— vast chambers cut out of the solid rock. Stern and forbidding without, the massive overhanging porticos casting deep shadows in the bright glare of a tropic sun, and dusky and dark within, lighted only by a stray sunbeam that might fall through the open door or by the traveller's torch. They are all empty now, for the mummies, with which time dealt so leniently, found no mercy at the hands of men. The coffins were rudely broken open in search of the gold ornaments which were often buried with the dead, and even the linen cloths in which the bodies were wrapped were taken off and sold for rags.

The interior of these rock-cut tombs was often ornamented in the most minute way—not only with hieroglyphics, but with colored drawings which still remain. They represented often, scenes in the life of the departed hero. In one place he is putting to flight his enemies, while in another, as a victor he is receiving captives who bend before him in supplication. On one of the oldest of these tombs is inscribed a funeral procession by water, where the mummy of the dead man is lying in a boat, which is followed by other boats full of mourning friends and kinsmen, while other friends are throwing dust upon their heads in token of grief.

When the hills were far distant from the

Interior of rock-cut Tomb.

river, as at Memphis, some different places of burial must be provided. Tombs were built beneath the surface of the ground, often of great extent, with large and massive chambers ornamented with hieroglyphics and drawings such as we have described. Besides these roomy chambers, pits were dug at intervals twenty or even seventy feet in depth, and around the sides were shelves of stone on which mummies were placed. The openings to these were closed with masonry which was removed when new bodies were to be introduced.

Of course the lowest class could afford no such costly burial as those we have described; their bodies washed only with some vegetable preparation, after lying in a strong alkali for seventy days, were wrapped in cloths, and laid away in pits in the plain.

In contrast with this humble burial stands out the magnificence of the royal sepulchres. The mighty pyramids are each the tomb of a single king. Their name pyramid comes from the union of two words *pi-rama*, the mountain, and though this may seem a somewhat high-sounding name for them, they are the largest buildings in the world. There are in Egypt some seventy pyramids, the majority of which are in the neighborhood of Memphis. Of these two are especially worthy of note.

The older of them is supposed to have been built by Cheops, who reigned over 2000 years before Christ. The second is the work of Chefren, and is of a later date, and owing to its standing on higher ground, appears to be of larger size than that of Cheops, though it is in reality not so high. The base of each

covers eleven acres of ground, while their height is nearly five hundred feet. Herodotus, the Greek historian, tells us that they were twenty years in building, and that one hundred thousand men, relieved every three months, were always at work upon them during that time. At his day there was still legible upon one of them an inscription to the effect that sixteen hundred talents of silver were spent upon the radishes, onions, and garlic for the workmen.

As we think of their enormous size, the patience and skill that created them seems almost incredible. First, the huge blocks must be hewn out in the distant quarry, and floated down the river. Then, as the pyramids stood back at a distance from its banks, they must be conveyed to them, and raised to their proper place. It is supposed that they were so moved by an inclined plane, which was raised as the work proceeded, and up which the heavy blocks were carried, and laid in their proper place. This inclined plain, or causeway, was still standing when Herodotus visited Egypt, and he speaks of its great proportions with admiration, considering it as in no respect inferior to the pyramids.

A narrow and intricate passage through this enormous mass of masonry led to a chamber situated nearly in the centre of the whole, where the mummy of the king was deposited. This chamber was ventilated by two very small passages or chimneys, which led upward, opening in the sides of the pyramid near its summit, and was ornamented in the most extravagant manner. After burial, the entrances were closed in the most careful way, so as to hide all evidence of their existence, and here the king hoped that his body would remain undisturbed till the spirit should come again to inhabit it. Vain hope! Not one of these tombs exists that has not been broken into. The cupidity of the Arabs and the curiosity of travellers have undone that result for which the hundred thousand workmen labored for so many years, and the bones of the kings are scattered far and wide.

MONUMENTS OF EGYPT.

Court of an Egyptian Temple.

CHAPTER IV.

CLOSE beside the pyramids of which we have been speaking, stands the Sphinx. Carved out of the solid rock, its giant proportions rise high above the plain of shifting sand in which it is half-buried. It bears the head of a man upon the body of a lion, and perhaps alone among the monuments of Egypt, is successful in concealing the secret of its creation. The Arabs call it Aboolhol, the father of terror or immensity. Its height from the belly to the head is fifty-six feet, while the circumference of the brows alone is over a hundred feet. Between its fore-paws is a chapel now buried in the sand. In this has been discovered a tablet, telling of repairs done to the statue by Suphis, the builder of the great pyramid.

This monarch lived more than two thousand years before Christ, and if the statue was then so old as to need repair, how far back must have been the date of its creation. A late traveller, in describing the Sphinx, has well said, "In one regard, this stone idol bears awful semblance of Deity—unchangefulness in the midst of change—the same

seeming will and intent, for ever and ever inexorable! Upon ancient dynasties of Ethiopian and Egyptian kings; upon Greek and Roman, upon Arab and Ottoman conquerors; upon Napoleon dreaming of an Eastern empire; upon battle and pestilence, upon keen-eyed travellers;—upon all, and more, this unworldly Sphinx has watched, and watched like a providence, with the same earnest eyes and the same sad, tranquil mien. And we, we shall die, and Islam wither away, and still that sleepless rock will lie watching and watching the works of the new busy race, with those same sad, earnest eyes, and the same tranquil mien everlasting."

A short distance only from the pyramids, near the river bank, we come to the site of the ancient and mighty city of Memphis, now marked only by a few fragments of stone and mummy pits.

Ascending the river from Memphis, we come, after a long journey, to the ruins of Thebes, the mightiest city of ancient Egypt. "Art thou mightier," cries Nahum the prophet, when denouncing Nineveh, "than populous No, that was situate among the rivers that had the waters round about it. Egypt and Ethiopia were her strength, and it was infinite."

When we think of it as it was, the greatest city of the earth for more than a thousand years, and picture it in its grandeur, with its hundreds of temples and monuments, and all the busy life of its inhabitants, and when now we see the plain on which it stood, scattered over with the remains of all this magnificence, we think again of the fiery words of Ezekiel the

Luxor from the river.

prophet. "Thus saith the Lord, I will set fire in Egypt, No shall be rent asunder."

The plain on which the city was built was one especially suited, as well by its beauty as its convenience, for the site of a great city. The hills which elsewhere lie close to the river, here fall back on either side, leaving a large circular plain.

The wealth of all Egypt was brought to its door on the broad bosom of the Nile, while it was, too, on the highway of the trade that was carried on with the ports on the Red sea.

Always a large populous city, its magnificence perhaps began under Amosis, who drove out of Egypt the Shepherd kings, a race of foreign tyrants who had held sway over the country and brought all Egypt under his rule. He was succeeded by a line of kings, each of whom brought fame and wealth to their capital, and who showed their piety in building massive temples to the gods. Finally, Thebes reached its greatest glory, under Rameses II., the great hero and the type of all that was noblest to the Egyptian. Then came the period of her downfall. The cities of Lower Egypt gained power, and later on an Ethiopian king conquered and ruled over the city. Then came the invasion by the Persians, with their hatred of everything Egyptian, and the mighty temples were ruined and thrown down by conquerors, who lost no opportunity to show the people that they were conquered, and who wished to destroy all evidence of the glorious deeds of their forefathers. Fortunately, they could not do this entirely, and so the ruins of Thebes to-day.

though only ruins, are the wonder and admiration of every one that sees them.

The site of the city is now marked by four villages, Luxor and Karnak on the eastern bank of the Nile, and Gurneh and Medineh Aboo on the western. At each of these places are ruins of great temples, and it seems as if each had been the chief point of its own district. Formerly the Nile did not, as now, flow through the centre of the city, but far to the eastward, leaving the plain, on which it was built, undivided. It is only within a few hundred years that it has forced for itself the channel it now uses, where it bids fair in a short time to work more destruction than centuries of neglect.

The Egyptian temples were built in a style of magnificence which any illustration can but poorly represent. They were often approached through a long avenue of sphinxes, called a dromos, of which but the broken fragments now remain. These led to a huge propylon, or gateway, behind which was an unroofed court, after traversing which the temple itself was reached. The massive pil-

Sphinx.

lars bore carvings representing the sacred lotus flower, or the graceful papyrus, and on every side were sculptures representing the hero who had built the temple, or the god in whose honor the temple was erected. In one place the god is shown delivering into the

Ruined Avenue of Sphinxes.

hands of his favorite the opposing army, while in another, the king is in battle, his enemies everywhere flying before him.

The accompanying cut, which is of a temple half buried by the sand, gives a good idea of the form which was generally chosen by the Egyptians in building their temples. On the right hand is the propylon; just left of it is the court, while still further to the left is the temple itself, or sanctuary.

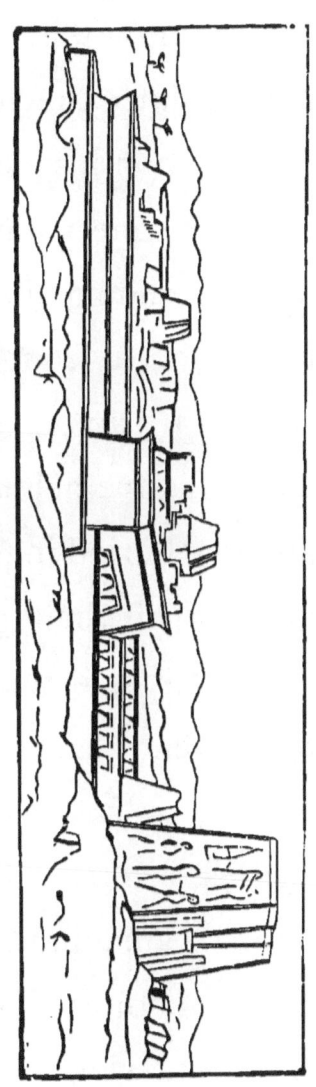

A very noticeable feature of Egyptian architecture is the high statues which form part of their temples. Sometimes the column that upholds a massive wall is carved into the form of a man, bearing the whole upon his head;—at other times, huge stone sentinels stand at the entrance keeping a never ending silent watch. Two such sentinels stand in front of the propylon of a ruined temple at Luxor. Their heads are surmounted with massive helmets, and though the figures are now buried in the sand up to their armpits, an idea of their great size may be gained, when it is said that the part still uncovered is over twenty feet in height.

But by far the most striking of these giant figures are the two Colossi, called by the Arabs Tama and Chama. They were erected by Amunopth III., who reigned about 1300 B. C., and were originally two out of eighteen such figures that formed the approach to a

Ramesside at Luxor.

temple. Their sixteen brothers, however, have disappeared, and they now stand alone. They are indeed giant in height, reaching sixty feet above the plain. From the elbow to the ends of the fingers, each arm is seventeen feet ten inches in length, while each sturdy foot measures ten feet.

One of these is the far-famed Memnon of the Greeks, and from it, it was fabled, a strain of music came when the first beams of the rising sun fell upon it. The cause of this music is unknown. Probably it was the work of the priests, who would lose no opportunity to impose upon the credulity of the ignorant, or it may be that it was owing, as has been suggested of late, to the expansion of particles of water in the stone under the warmth of the sun's rays. The Persians did not spare these any more than the other examples of

Egyptian greatness, and it is only from the mutilated remains that we can judge how stately must have been the perfect originals.

We have a very vivid picture on an old wall, of a colossus in process of transportation. The huge figure is firmly bound upon a sledge with ropes, and is drawn by four long lines of laborers, each line being made up of forty-three men. One man stands upon the knees of the statue, apparently giving out some song, or beating time, that all may pull together. On the sledge stands another man pouring from a vase some substance, evidently grease, in order to assist locomotion; while bands of laborers follow with tools and a body of soldiers march by the side.

During the inundation, the water completely surrounds the Colossi, which then rise like two great islands of stone above the flood.

Indeed, their bases are now already covered, seven feet in depth, with the mud which successive overflows of the river have deposited. It is well known that the bed of the river is slowly rising, since within the positive knowledge of history, the floods extend to points far beyond their former reach, and there is reason to believe that when these statues were erected, the ground on which they stood was never reached by the yearly overflow, and that it is only during comparatively late centuries, that the waters have extended to their present limit.

Crossing the river from Luxor, we find on the opposite side at a short distance from its bank, the ruins of what was one of the grandest of all the Egyptian temples. Diodorus, the Greek historian, describes it, calling it the tomb of Osymandyas. "At its entrance," says he, "rose a propylon of marble. After having passed it, one entered a square court, whose roof was not sustained by columns but by animals carved in solid blocks of stone. The entire ceiling, consisting of a single stone, was studded with golden stars upon a field of azure. At the further end of this court was a second propylon, like the former but adorned with variegated carvings of perfect workmanship. Beside this second portico were three statues, each chiselled from a single block of the hard and tinted stones of Syene. One, representing a personage in a sitting posture, was the largest of all the statues in Egypt. This piece was not only remarkable for its dimensions, but it was worthy of admiration in regard to its artistic execution and the nature of the stone which, notwithstanding its vastness, did not reveal a single crack or blemish.

Ruins of Temple of Rameses.

Upon it could be read the following inscription, 'I am Osymandyas, king of the kings; if any one should wish to know who I am, and where I repose, let him surpass one of my works.' The two other statues placed near his knees, one upon the right hand and the other upon the left, were those of the mother and daughter, and did not approach the first in size.

"Upon a wall near at hand, the king was represented besieging a fortress surrounded by a river, exposing himself to the blows of his enemies, and accompanied by a terrible lion, which served him as an auxiliary in his combats. Among those who explain these carvings, some say that it was a real lion, tamed, fed by the king's own hands, and taught to accompany him while attacking and pursuing his enemies; while others maintain that this king, who was distinguished above all the rest for his valor and strength, intended to sound his own praises by symbolizing his qualities in the figure of a lion."

One large apartment was doubtless the library, for above its doorway was inscribed, " Books are the medicine of the mind."

At the back and sides of the building are vaults of unburned bricks, which were probably used as dwelling places for the priests. A few of higher rank no doubt lived nearer the sanctuary, and to these was assigned the duty of offering sacrifices to attain the favor of the deities on behalf of the nation.

Such was this temple. It was erected by Rameses II., to his father Oimenepthah, or Osymandyas, as Diodorus calls him. Not only was it perfect in workmanship, but its situation was one of great beauty. Built just at

the foot of a range of hills, its different parts were raised on successive terraces, thus making its outward appearance particularly massive.

The giant statue is still there, but like everything about it, in ruins. It lies prone on its face, but even in its downfall is the wonder of all. Its huge mass weighs nearly nine hundred tons, and modern engineering skill would, we fear, be sorely tasked, if it were called upon to transport such a figure from the quarries at Syene, hundreds of miles distant, and set it upright in its place in the temple.

Such were some of the great monuments of Egypt. The drifting sands of the desert have buried other temples and tombs out of our sight, and their memory is forgotten. It is as if nature, having in vain striven to destroy these works of man through the long years that have elapsed since their creation, had given up the unequal struggle, and was now resolved to bury them out of her sight. The shifting sand may yet do what time has not, and the remains of ancient Egypt may thus finally disappear.

www.ingramcontent.com/pod-product-compliance
Lightning Source LLC
Chambersburg PA
CBHW030905170426
43193CB00009BA/738